SEASONS

Robert Sieviec

Burlington,
Vermont

Onion River Press
Burlington, VT 05401

info@onionriverpress.com
www.onionriverpress.com

ISBN: 978-1-957184-56-2

Library of Congress Control Number: 2024905143

SPRING (WETU)

Snow melts like a receding tide, exposing mud, debris,
Cigarette butts until now suspended in snowbanks.
Birds already comb patchy grass for thawing insects.

Sidewalks warm, winter layers are shed: Mud season! Wear your Wellingtons!
Eyes unfocus in the warm breeze, sun softens to a golden blur.
The first cardinal sings his mating song; woodpeckers peck.

Remembered spring floods memory: feelings of hope, joy, love.
Feelings, sadly, we may never know again,
Reserved as they are for the young, mostly, as spring ghosts us.

April snow, winter's parting shot; still, enjoy this spring, another one seen.
Come high summer, amnesia season, we'll be sunning ourselves like
Reptiles on rocks, heat-dazed, spring forgotten.

MORNING OF ANOTHER DAY

Morning of another day, birdsong on the breeze
Rustles the leaves in the trees
The light shines through.
Morning of another day with you.

Looking up the sky is blue,
Looking down the grass is green.
In between life goes on like a dream.
One day we'll awaken and we'll be gone.

Some things are meant to last as long as life.
One thing that will last is our love.

Morning of another day, birdsong on the breeze
Rustles the leaves in the trees
The light shines through.
Morning of another day with you.

THE CRASH

When I was eight I witnessed a car crash
On a dangerous curve in front of my house.
I ran from the backyard and saw a teenage girl lying
On her side on the ground, one arm folded under her,
The other extended out, eyes closed, lips parted,
Long hair flowing on the grass.

But for a bruise on her cheek, she looked to be asleep
Instead of dead. Neighbors who came on the scene to help
Stepped carefully around her maybe knowing instinctively
That she was gone: half in, half out of the passenger side,
Feet still in the foot-well of the car that had horseshoed around a tree
That, not for the first time, had been a magnet for speeding cars.
The teenage driver behind the wheel cried out in agony,
Pinned by the steering column.

A premature sibling had died the year before my brother and I were born
And was buried in a section of graveyard reserved for infants,
Headstones with cherubs.
Our family would visit the grave around which my father
Had put up a miniature white picket fence, until one year
A nearby river rose up in flood and washed it away, along with
Many other graves of lives just begun lost, like this teenage girl's.

Long or short, life seems the exception,
Death the rule. We are sparks thrown off by a fire
Raging in eternity.

THE LUCASES

Miye onagu itatowata onajin.
(I stand upwind of burnt prairie, burnt bridges behind me.)

I remember a Scottish couple,
John and Ann Lucas, family acquaintances,
Ann, especially of my mother, with whom
She'd converse in Gaelic when she wanted
To unburden herself without my knowing what was being said.
John worked with my father.

My mother, brother and I would flee to their place
When our father was in a rage.
There it was as if we were no longer in the States but
In Edinburgh or Glasgow.
There was proper tea and Scottish shortbread in tins,
Orange marmalade on English muffins.

Their home seemed all but
Transported whole from Scotland.
We slept in beds beneath quilted covers,
Stepped onto cold floors in the morning,
Sat in overstuffed armchairs in front of a
Roaring fire in a stone fireplace.

When John died, a bolt of lightning struck the church at his funeral.
A sign if ever there was, I felt, that his passing was noteworthy.

Back at their home, his son and daughter received mourners.
I remember watching his son, a U.S. naval officer,
Thinking about his father as he held a ring that had belonged to him.
I envied him.

We part, each of us off on our own course,
In time coming to the shores of the same sea.
Per the law of conservation: Matter can neither be created
Nor destroyed, only transformed.

You bring out what you brought in.

ON PEARL STREET

I came across a pearl on Pearl Street: a young woman sleeping in a doorway
Beneath a thin white blanket, her bare feet sticking out onto the sidewalk,
Her belongings arrayed behind her to the closed door.

Her hands were curled beside her head.
It was mid-morning on an already soon-to-be hot day;
Ever hotter in the new climate.

I thought, she must be exhausted to be able to sleep in the heat.
Maybe she was on her way to getting used to the changing climate,
As we all must soon.

I took out a bill and let it flutter into her belongings, hopefully safe until
She awakens, finds it and uses it to buy a cold drink, something to eat.
Sleep, daughter, sleep. May you dream better dreams.

FAMILY RESTAURANT

Dutch Mill, Friendly's, IHOP:
Eating out at the family restaurant.
Your children when they were young,
You being broken into parental harness.

Booths to slide across, cruets of flavored maple syrups,
Eggs over easy, hash browns, home fries,
Always full pots of coffee,
Heavy china plates and mugs, kitchen aroma.

It's said the sense of smell evokes the strongest memories,
Our own canine sense cataloging our experiences.
Memories surface, then drop again like stones in water.

Occasionally they resurface so strongly that,
For a moment, you feel you're there again,
All of you, in happier times.
Nostalgia washes over you, like endorphins

The brain floods the dying animal with,
Easing its suffering at the end.
In the expanding universe
We grow further and further apart.

PANDEMIC

Courtland Hill to Highland Park: Ten years stasis since coming to rest.
Regrets on an emptied life mount as do deaths
While sheltering in place.
Viral change approaches, coming in waves.

Politicians grasp at straws.
Money is found to pay billionaire rentiers.
Bread and circuses are suspended for now,
The Red Death inside Prospero's palace.

Nature creeps back into spaces temporarily
Abandoned by man: sky and water clear.
We'll have to take our chances when we return:
In the soup, so to speak, while awaiting a cure, everything unsure.

Black lives are taken, cities erupt in protest.
Prospero flails about in his bunker, his contempt for the law exposed.
There has never been a moment more evident
When those who rule us don't care or know how.
Treason, I say. Treason most high.

The future is masked: the herd being culled for
Those who'll live in the new normal.
Nostalgia plays hard now, the golden age slipping away.
Time has slowed down, mere months since it began.

When do we restart the consumer culture?
When can we resume ravaging the planet?
When will we learn that if there's one thing
We can be certain of in life, it's uncertainty?

We lie between before and after, then and the unfolding future;
Between the end of history and the new world to come.
The old gives way to the new, the long-awaited moment.

Until then ...

Four AM the robins begin to sing their encoded song:
I am here, I am here, I am here.
Mayan ruins, lost 'til now, are mapped from space:
Works of man, works of man, works of man.

Past presages future; jellyfish swim in Venetian canals.
Incantate: We were here, we were here, we were here.
World without end.
Amen.

BIG TUJUNGA FIRE (1975)

Fallout-like Pompeian ash, burnt-leaf New England fall aroma,
Red sun at noon, unnatural cloud,
A forest goes up like tissue paper.

At its edges fighters fight, while flare-ups shoot out of the
Already consumed zone, the core still hot
Where winds fan embers into flame.

The ghost of fire plays on its surface,
Ashes glow brightly, cooling all the while.

HAIKUS (I)

The sky, a river,
Having poured rain down the street,
Became cloudless blue

Stand still in your place
And listen to how it sounds
Without you in it

Ice forms a prism
On the window refracting
Diamond-patterned light

LOCKDOWN – 3/18/20

Spring snow sprung on us
Sheltering in place: nowhere
To go anyway

Dew evaporates
From a meadow never touched
By developers

SUMMER (BLOKETU)

The sound of distant lawnmowers, the smell of new-mown grass;
Cardinals chitter beneath the temperate forest canopy; crickets sing
In the cool summer night; lush green insect-pollinated landscape;
The smell of damp earth between passing showers.

Trees are green, crops grow, rivers run.
A memory: sitting beneath a tree's spreading branches
On a grassy hillside, wind rippling
A sea of grass below next to a white barn and silo.
Where was that?

A Buffalo & Pittsburgh engine, the "Mortimer B. Fuller III",
Pulls Burlington Electric woodchip cars resembling coal hoppers
Day and night on the railroad behind me.

One hundred-thirteen years ago, trains pulled into the siding here
Carrying supplies for, products from, the factory my apartment building
Once was. Perhaps the red brick building holds the ghosts of long-dead
Workers who picnicked on the grounds in past summers.

Warm rain. A cardinal alights on a stockade fence.
F35s scream overhead ... two, four, six, eight.
Time dilates...
The young are everywhere.

L.A. LULLABY

You're an island of thought, adrift in the Santa Anas
Driving down Pacific Coast Highway.
Going day to day with your loved one,
The two of you between the mountains and the ocean.

Funny how you can't wish you were someplace else, far away.
Being an island of thought, adrift in the Santa Anas,
And tomorrow's another day.

The dying palms sway in the Santa Anas.
The sun dives behind an orange cloud.
Tonight the California moon's a sliver.
The air cold enough to shiver.

Funny how you can't wish you were someplace else, far away.
Being an island of thought, adrift in the Santa Anas,
And tomorrow's another day.
And tomorrow's another day.

CRAZY HORSE RIDES AGAIN

(Tašunke Witko šunkakanyanka ake)

As small western towns disappear, prairie grows, buffalo roam,
I imagine Crazy Horse riding again.
Avoid foreign entanglements, that time is past and done.
Now's the time for summing up all the wisdom that you've won.

Don't mind cold if I have stars,
Being alone and not break another heart,
Helping out when things fall apart,
Helping make a fresh start.

A man who could've been my father
Told me what his told him.
He said, 'You become a man when you're reconciled
To necessity.'

What I want I can't have.
What I need I might get.
What I must do I do
Without hope or regret.

As small western towns disappear,
Prairie grows, buffalo roam,
I imagine Crazy Horse riding,
Riding again.

JOSEPHINE

There's a photograph over a hundred years old, hanging on my wall,
On the back of which my mother scribbled 'Josephine, astride my horse Folly.'
Josephine was one of my mother's older sisters, she being the youngest of
Four girls and two boys.

Sitting astride Folly atop an English saddle, feet in English stirrups,
Josephine appears to be about six or seven years old.
A man in suit, tie and cap holds the reins – maybe her father, maybe not.
An ivy-covered manor house is in the background.

My mother's father was caretaker of an English-owned estate.
When he died my grandmother and her six children were evicted:
No caretaker, no domicile.
The girls went to convents; the boys I don't know where.
They would reunite later on in life.

The years passed: my mother went into nursing;
Served in London during the Blitz;
Came to America, married, started a family.
Josephine did likewise.

However, it was Josephine who should have been my mother; I, her son.
We were two peas in a pod, as the saying goes.
She sussed me out for smoking when she gave me a cigarette
When I was thirteen and watched me light up.

('Oh, yeah', she said. 'He knows how to smoke.')
Years later, in hospital, dying of lung cancer, my mother in attendance,
Josephine and I were alone in her hospital room.
I said to her, 'I love you'
And she said, 'I love you, too.'

I would smoke a million cigarettes to get to see her now.

William Faulkner wrote, 'The past isn't dead. It isn't even past yet.'
And the pull of the past is very strong.
I do not believe Jesus was the Son of God, although his teachings still hold true.
I do not believe in heaven or hell, but maybe there is a God.

But if believing would allow me to see Josephine again,
I would consider doing so.

FACE ON A COIN

If I were emperor of Rome, I'd put your face on a coin.
Hold your timeless beauty in my hand, in silver, in gold.

If I were emperor of France, you'd be my Josephine;
Back in Paris while I conquer the world for you.

But I only get to watch you playing with your lovers' hearts,
Looking for the first fault line.
Them never knowing they were losing from the start all the time.

If I were the king of hearts, you'd be the queen.
I'd do anything for you if you'd only ask me.

But I only get to see you playing with your lover's heart,
Looking for the first fault line.
Him never knowing he was losing from the start all the time.

If I were emperor of Rome, I'd put your face on a coin.
Hold your timeless beauty in my hand, in silver, in gold.
If I were emperor, if I were your lover.

CANYON

The canyon between buildings is cool.
Birds sing in parking garage tiers above.
A concrete walkway runs along the bottom, connecting backways.
A war party could easily slip through.

This trail has been trod before.
Many ghosts pass, taking the fight to the enemy.
Where are today's warriors?
To whom will the sachems pass power?

Everywhere the Great Herd roams the planet.
Some are led blindly off cliffs, but the main herd thunders past.
This trail has been trod before, and must be followed to its end.
Along the way, we must act honorably at all times.

The powers that be must see they are as trapped as the rest of us,
That we all became distracted primates, seeking shiny baubles.
If it's in our nature, there's no point in vengeance.
We have all plundered the planet. Now we must try to repair it.

Was the road that led here inevitable? Is it something in life itself?
A pattern through time: survive, thrive, fill every niche, use everything up?
Is it too late to turn things around? Maybe.
But we are here for those who follow, so we must try.

Crazy Horse, Tašunke Witko, said all the young of the world
Would come together one day to save maka, the earth.
Today's warriors are everywhere.
The time is now. Crazy Horse rides again.
Tašunke Witko šunkakanyanka ake.

Meanwhile, back in the canyon:
Lake breeze, imagining the smell of salt.
Canadian smoke.
Leaf shadow.
Pine needles.
Sunlit path.
Purpose.
Repose.
Rebirth.

HAIKUS (II)

Like the expanding
Universe, we grow further
And further apart

We never left the
Garden of Eden, and Eve
Is restoring it

Cold air poured through the
Window like a waterfall
Over the sleeper

(GETTING OLD)

Frequent stops at park
Benches like Stations of the
Cross: bend, kneel, pray, rise

We are sparks thrown off
By a fire raging in
Eternity

FALL (PTANYELA)

An arrow of geese –
A dozen forming the head.
A dozen more the shaft –
Flies south, honking noisily.

The setting sun lances across rooftops,
Through nearly leafless trees,
Sinking further toward winter solstice.
Beneath its rays houses sit in shadow.

Gray skies greet gray days
In the gray season.
The cardinal couple outside my window are
Visible among the branches

Of low, berried trees, picking at fruit.
Once hidden amidst greenery,
They're exposed now.
What else is exposed now?

Trees stiffen, sap slows; fauna retreat to
Winter sleep, dreaming of spring and summer
Until they awaken.

TWO HAWKS (Nunpa Cetan)

Two hawks spun 'round each other above me
In a cloudless blue sky.
"Cetan," I said.

I had just stepped out of a store and saw them
Approaching, fifty feet up, wings spread motionless,
Moving east in a strong wind.

I saw their eyes, their hooked yellow beaks,
Their feathers rippling in the wind.
They circled each other and were soon lost from sight.

I retraced my steps to see how I'd arrived
At precisely the right moment to witness their passage.
Where did I go? What did I do? Was it just coincidence?

Or had they found me?

I suppose it depends upon your point of view.
Maybe the natural world reaches out to us,
From time to time,

To remind us of our place in it;
Of the consequences of our actions on it;
And the woes it can visit upon us.

Or maybe it's supremely indifferent to the fate we bring upon ourselves.

Wapetokeca owakita.
Watch for sign.
Watch for sign.

SYLVIA (for Sylvia Plath)

Sylvia, when I hear your voice I feel it calling me home,
Reminding me of how soon we're gone.
How much longer now I'm done?

Do you remember the first time the muse touched you?
A touch of the poet, in time, can undo.
Trauma from the past can haunt our future too much.
I dig deeply as you did, risking losing touch.

Did you mistake a gray day for one you thought black?
The fog thickens, then it thins, but it never will roll back.
Sylvia, when I hear your voice I feel it calling me home.

You were gone long before I found you,
Prematurely, preordained or both.
But you live on inside me, paradoxically giving me hope.

Did you mistake a gray day for one you thought black?
The fog thickens, then it thins, but it never will roll back.

Sylvia, when I hear your voice I feel it calling me home,
Reminding me of how soon we're gone.
How much longer now I'm done?

A PERFECT DAY

Blue sky dome; wind soughing through
Trees, green branches waving;
Cooler now between harvest moon and
Start of autumn.

Things fall into place:
Bus connections synchronize;
A long sought-after book
Appears on a bookseller's shelf;

A call comes in regarding housing
(You're next),
Karma flows high and good.
Hope grows.

Painter's light throws
Everything in stark relief:
Colors brighten, shadows lengthen.
Max Parrish-like golden light suffuses all.

On an otherworldly day like today
You can imagine your life different:
Fuller, happier, more meaningful, more purposeful;
At one with nature, with God even.

And despite dark, sinking thoughts,
Distant loved ones, loneliness and
Old age, the paradisal view of
A perfect day remains.

A HEART BREAKS LIKE ICE AT THE EDGE

A heart breaks like ice at the edge, falls into the sea.
Keeps on coming, coming back to me.
Nothing is what it means – you fall apart and come together
Again and again and again,
And the more it seems …

You only know what you know, you don't know nothing.
Only something's missing you can't put your finger on.
Remember when if you still go back seeking something lost
You can't get back – true friends or a love so fine,
You couldn't find the time.

There is no time; place is always and only place.
Running out of places to go to, people to turn to,
Faces to don, wondering when it's gonna dawn.

It's always twelve-thirty-four when I glance at the clock.
Counting up or down I wonder which?
Your heart is like a red, red rose bleeding in my hand,
I love you to death.

As never was meant to be, no good deed goes unpunished.
Act nobly, wait and see.
For hidden, selfish reasons I make things worse instead of better.

Can't have what I want, get what I need.
All I do is make you bleed.
Don't mean to hurt you but then it's true –
The ones you love you always do.

Some things seem farther away than the moon,
More remote than China.
Holding true, holding you.

MY FATHER'S HANDS

I splashed some boiling water on my hands the other day while making tea.
I ignored the burning sensation, thinking of how my father's hands exhibited
All the burns, bangs, scarifications of a lifetime spent in the Navy,
Manufacturing, welding.

My father worked six days a week with overtime,
Paid off the mortgage within fifteen years,
Had a motorboat to cruise and fish Long Island Sound,
To take him back onto the waters he'd learned to love
While serving in World War Two.

I would hear him beneath my window, opening the garage door at 6AM,
Starting his car, backing up the driveway, closing the garage door,
Then going off to another twelve-hour workday.
I, along with my brother, had lain still in our room until he'd gone
And then we could breathe again.

Once, on an earlier version of take-your-kids-to-work day,
He brought us onto the factory floor where he and his coworkers
Manufactured the world's goods while living the American dream.
There were red-brick buildings, food trucks on the adjoining streets.
American-made cars filled the parking lots.

The last time I went down those streets it looked like Berlin, 1945.

When he died it was both sad and a relief: loss in that
I'd never really got to know him, if we ever get to know anyone.
Too late to learn the lessons he could have taught me that

I had to learn myself "the hard way," as he used to say.
If there's any other way.
My mother told me when my father died three men had to replace him
To do the work he'd done.

The Nazis said you could tell who were Jews by their soft hands,
Having never done hard work in their lives.
Louis B. Mayer, before he went to Hollywood to help found MGM,
Worked in his father's ship-salvaging and scrap-iron business.
There was nothing soft about him.

I wish I had my father's hands.

UVALDE

In Uvalde:
An eleven-year-old girl saw her teacher shot dead in front of her
('Goodnight!');
Survived the shooting by smearing a dead friend's blood on
Herself so as to appear dead;
Called 911 on a dead teacher's cellphone;
And agreed to an off-camera interview with CNN
On one condition: No men.

If I were a woman I would say to all women
Remember that.
Run with it.
No men.
Men have a long way to go to get back into
Women's good graces.

WINTER (WANIYETU)

Snow: cold, clean, quiet;
Summer's obverse, winter white;
Mirror of the mind.

'Go north,' a voice says
'Go colder 'til the whiteness
Comes to collect you.'

'Go where snow still falls,
Preparing yourself for the
Warming world to come.'

Once, traveling south,
Snow flew past the train window
Like sunlit diamonds.

Ice shelves broke up on
Riverbanks collapsing into
The spring current.

All that may end soon
As summer waxes longer,
Winter wanes sooner.

While polar bears face
Extinction, we will begin
Yachting the Arctic.

We have lost our way
Back to the natural world
Pursuing profit.

Snow: cold, clean, quiet;
Summer's obverse, winter white;
Mirror of the mind.

6AM

At 6AM the flashing red/yellow traffic lights resume their normal pattern.
The lake beyond is gray, the distant shore a white line 'neath the Adirondacks.
The breeze is cool, an updraft, gulls riding it offshore.
A runner enters the park and runs downhill on the biking/running path.
An early-to-work pedestrian crosses the street.
The facade of the hotel opposite betrays nothing about its guests.
The overcast light gray sky has strips of darker gray and white clouds in it.
There's the calm before the day's predicted storms.

IRRETRIEVABLE

So long together, thought it would last forever;
Started hopeful, now irretrievable.
Memory will haunt with clarity,
Heartache with love's lost intensity.
All that was possible, now irretrievable.

If I could make the bad times good, I would.
Good times seem even better.
Erase the pain of wasted time,
Make beginning again not irretrievable.

Days grow short, but know before time runs out,
My love for you was never in doubt.
And 'though it's too late, not irretrievable.
And 'though it's too late, not irretrievable.

GHOSTS

I dreamt my father's ghost last night, standing in the hall

Of the house he built I grew up in.

Wrapped in a blanket with all the lights on in all the rooms,

He peered into each as if asking himself, 'Where did I go wrong? Why?'

I put my hand on his shoulder and said,

'I do the same thing, too,' as we looked into the rooms of his house

For the ghosts of his family,

And I looked into mine for mine.

Sorrowing over what was gone,

What could never be relived better again,

I watched him fade away, walking through his rooms.

I turned off the lights in mine and faded into

Wakefulness to write this down.

ISOLATE (ISə,LIT)

Alone, bewildered, marooned, the end begins.

Dead friends' possessions lie as lifeless as my own will one day.

Rituals comfort the living still clinging to life.

In dreams I breakfast with ghosts who say to me,

'Give up the ghosts of things you should've long ago. Manage yourself!

We were never going to be of any help.'

Everything is metered, timed just so.

Hold on until it's time to let go.

I can feel a semi-cool summer night and

Hear crickets on a patio long ago.

Collapse the continuum, conclude the experiment.

The child no longer cries; demons enjoy well-deserved rest.

Thunderheads of the past roll away in the distance.

Alone, bewildered, marooned, the end begins.

Survival, emptiness, silence, stillness.

But in the stillness eternity gently enfolds us.

WOCEKIYE	PRAYER
Miye cekiye …	I pray …
Cantiyozikiya	Be calm
Iyasny	Become still
Hohošni	Silent
Nihanyanšni	Don't be afraid
Cantet'inza	Be brave
Woheyata iyeya	Push back
Wawat'ecayanka	Be gentle
Akoza wowahwala	Try kindness
Wowahwacin	Desire peace
Wowacintanka	Persevere
Iyotan wašte ape	Hope for the best
K'oyela wašte lehanyan	All good thus far (so far, so good)
Nita cangku awanyanka	See to your own path
Cekiye, cekiye …	Pray, pray …

ABSOLUTE ZERO

I approach absolute zero: -273°C, -460°F, 0° Kelvin.
No heat, no motion; time passes glacially,
The frozen past observable.

Living rock thrusts out of the ground in front of which
The young family takes pictures of itself before the
Terrible sadness that would descend upon them.

Father, mother, twins: 'Two for the one we buried,' said the mother.
Count the living, not the dead.
Have hope, not dread.

Father and twins sit together: the one on his right looks down,
The one on his left looks left at…what?
The road of earliest memory?

Tree branches moving in the breeze? A passing car?
What do we remember? Is all of it archived inside each of us?
And what about what happened?

Was it always meant to be the way it turned out?
In what alternate universe was it different, better?
Why did all the continuums collapse into only one inescapable one?

If you could enter the moment, could you issue a warning?
Do this, don't do that. Pause, let the moment of greatest danger,
Deja vu'd, pass. Do nothing until it's safe.

Or does everyone's past spill into their future,
Creating inevitabilities that can't be avoided,
Only played out, like a hand you're dealt, fate.

There is no knowing, there is no going back.
There is only regret and sadness, and
Forgiveness for what couldn't be helped.

Absolute zero: no heat, no motion.
Frozen riddles of the past.
Frozen heart, peace at last.